I HURT INSIDE

I HURT INSIDE

*A Christian Psychologist Helps
You Understand and Overcome
Feelings of Fear, Frustration,
and Failure*

Ralph C. Underwager

AUGSBURG PUBLISHING HOUSE
MINNEAPOLIS, MINNESOTA

I HURT INSIDE

Copyright © 1973 Augsburg Publishing House

Library of Congress Catalog Card No. 72-90265

International Standard Book No. 0-8066-1312-2

Manufactured in the United States of America

Contents

Preface

I hurt inside.

In my experience as a pastor and a clinical psychologist I have often heard others express in feelings, actions, and words, "I hurt inside."

The feeling of psychological pain is universal. We all feel the hurts of life deep inside ourselves. We may try extreme or mild measures to deal with our feelings of hurt, but we know we must handle our hurts in some way, even if we cannot understand them.

This book is intended to help you understand why you hurt inside and to offer help in overcoming your psychological pain.

In addition to my studies and experience in the fields of pastoral ministry and clinical psychology I have learned much about human psychological pain from the findings of A Study of Generations. This major research project on the beliefs, values, attitudes, and opinions of one large Christian denomination found basically two groups of people.

One group are those who tend to live life according to rules. They tend to measure their own worth and success by how well they believe they live up to the rules as they understand them. The term "law-oriented" describes this group.

The second group know the rules and standards, but they also recognize their human imperfection. They do not measure their worth by their performance record but by the grace and acceptance they believe God has given them in the Gospel of Jesus Christ. These are "gospel-oriented" people.

What does this have to do with "hurting inside" and "psychological pain"?

In this book I describe persons who have suffered various kinds of psychological pain. Each case is an illustration of an individual whose psychological pain is caused by a "law-oriented" life, the attempt to match an impossible standard, to live a perfect life to feel worthy and acceptable.

My first purpose in using these examples is to help you understand your own hurt and its cause. But merely to help you understand is not enough.

My ultimate purpose is to help you live in the confidence that God forgives, loves, and accepts you in Jesus Christ.

I Hurt Inside: Why?

A pastor said, "The most tragic and painful experience in my ministry was when I visited a faithful and loyal man of my congregation. He had had a stroke. Here was a strong, successful man who loved his Lord, had served the church for years, was in church every Sunday. He lay sobbing in the hospital bed. Between the sobs, clinging to my hand, he told me the reason for his anguish. He had forgotten to bring his prayer book to the hospital and so he couldn't pray." Without his prayer book he felt he was out of touch with God.

A young attractive couple finally had a baby girl after seven years of trying. This represented the fulfillment of some of their deepest hopes and needs. At first they were radiantly happy. After six months the wife became deeply depressed. She had many severe headaches, cried a great deal, lost weight, and neglected herself and her family. The emotional demands placed upon her by her own expectations about the way she should be as a mother paralyzed her.

A father who had worked hard for years building a plumbing business, nurturing the dream that his son would work with him one day, kicked his teen-age son out of the home. For years the father had held down his fear that his son was homosexual. The boy had never been interested in sports, spent much time alone, didn't show much interest in plumbing or girls. He was different and stayed different in spite of years of cajoling, threat, rewarding, and punishment. When the boy began to spend evenings with his high school math teacher, that was too much for the father. He blew up. He called the son "queer" and threw him out. The father could not tolerate any deviation, any difference from "other kids." He didn't know his son had an IQ of 150 and was a mathematical whiz. He could not accept the fact of his son being different from other boys.

A teen-age girl attempted suicide by taking about 100 aspirin. This was a serious signal to the parents that she was really hurting. She felt she was not pretty enough and didn't have enough dates. The parents had trouble accepting the fact that their daughter had tried suicide. They covered it up. They didn't talk about it beyond saying, "What would your grandparents say if . . . ? What would your friends say if . . . ?" The second time the girl used barbiturates. They worked. Neither the daughter nor the parents could cope with the feelings of inadequacy caused by their conviction that they did not meet the demands of society.

Psychological Pain Really Hurts

These kinds of events really happen. People hurt. I hurt. You hurt. There is a great plenty of human pain, enough for everybody. There are, of course, different kinds of pain. There is the physical pain of grief in the face of death. There is the pain of watching your children starve while you sit helpless in the midst of war or poverty. There is the pain of a cosmic bellyache when we feel that the problems of the world — peace, plenty and poverty, pollution, population — are just too great for any hope of solution. Then we wonder what life is for, what purpose there is to it all.

In this book I am not directly concerned with physical pain, pain associated with our mortality, the inequities of the social structure, or grand philosophical anxieties. To attempt to cover the whole range of human pain would be too large a task. I will deal with the kind of pain most familiar to all of us — the inner, personal sense of hurt that is primarily psychological in nature. Psychological pain is the kind of pain felt in the four real-life situations described above. You might call it garden variety, routine, everyday kind of pain. Yet its persistent and pervasive effects powerfully shape our lives and our experience, even if they are not as dramatic as the examples.

Many instances of psychological pain, of course, are less severe or extreme than others. There is the nervous housewife who finds that her blueberry pie is soft and runny when her husband's family is over for Thanksgiving. There is the shy teen-ager who has milk poured on his head in the school lunch room. There is the pain of a proud owner whose new car turns out to be a lemon. Most of us manage to handle such individual instances of psychological pain without breaking down. We get over the feeling of being hurt and go on. These are examples of the same kind of pain — inner, personal, daily, and often cumulative. Feelings of this pain add up or even multiply. This kind of pain affects our self-concept, our understanding of the world we live in, and our sense of purpose or direction in life. It affects our relationships with other persons, especially our family. Relationships can go sour along with everything else. This is the kind of pain that most frequently leads to those times when we say to ourselves, "Life is hell!"

We feel hurt and pain many times and in many ways. We become depressed or angry. Life feels so boring or painful that it seems intolerable. We want to run away, change jobs or towns, find new friends, get out of a bad marriage, or run away from cruel and heartless parents. We search for "true" friends with whom we can honestly share our feelings. We settle for a fleeting contact with a bartender or taxi driver. We may plunge into the equally transitory but more chic world of sensitivity training or encounter weekends. We may purchase the services of a professional friend in psychotherapy if we have enough money. Some may settle on the deceptive camaraderie of shared chemicals, either alcohol or psychoactive drugs. The hurt and pain generally continue.

All of us at times feel that life is grim and bleak. Those times may come and go, alternating with periods of calm and euphoria. Periods of contentment may be long or short, rhythmic or capricious. For some persons such periods of joy diminish until the times of pain merge into one long skein of gray numbness interrupted by an occasional twinge of sharp pain that is almost pleasant just because it is different. When that happens, a person may truly feel that life is hell. He thinks, "Hell is the most terrible thing there is. There cannot be anything more terrible than what is happening to me right now. Therefore, my life is hell."

That is right.

That life experience *is* hell.

Hell is to be apart from God. To be apart from God is to be under the accusing, judging, and condemning power of the law.

The Cause of Psychological Pain

To be under the law is to experience life as a demand. The demand is fundamentally that *I should be something other than what I am.* The church believes that God relates to the world and to men in two ways — through the law and through the gospel. All men by their nature and by their very existence encounter and know the law. In the church, Christians know and encounter the gospel that supersedes the law and gives a new relation to God. Men who know and encounter only the law know only a God of wrath and punishment. Those who know the gospel know a gracious God who sent Jesus Christ to free men from the curse of the law. Those who know only the law and only a wrathful God feel only the demand of the law, "Be different from what you are."

No matter who or what I am, that demand is always there. I have to be something else, something better, bigger, smarter, richer, more loving or loved. Name any dimension, any attribute, any capacity, any skill. The demand is still the same. Be more of this or less of that.

This constant demand is the source of psychological pain, of the feeling that sometimes life feels like hell. Fortunately for our psychological state, most of us are neither very good theologians nor very mature Christians. If we were and could rightly understand the sting of the law we would know true despair until the grace of God triumphed anew. As poor theologians and babies in Christ we manage to tame the law a little. We can delude ourselves for a time that the demand is met if we are good boys and girls. When that delusion doesn't hold up anymore we experience the pain for a time until we convince ourselves again that we really are not so bad. At least we can think of other people who are worse.

Externalizing the Cause and Cure

The defense we build against the law and its demands is to externalize both the cause and the cure. The *cause* of the pain is externalized when we believe that other people and outside events cause us to be unhappy or hurt us. This habit of belief is enshrined and encased in our language habits. "You make me so mad when...." "It really hurts me when you...." "I can't stand it when things go wrong...." "If only you would...." "Why can't you understand...." This is where the urge to flee the situation or the persons comes about. We are convinced that if we could just change the people or places around us we could be happy. We do not recognize that the unhappiness we feel comes largely, though not entirely, from inside us.

The *cure* of the pain is externalized when we make any type of structure or person outside of ourselves the source of meaning in life. Structures can be elevated into gods and frozen into unchanging shapes. Such a structure might be repeated patterns of behavior, i.e., the order of worship or our daily jobs. It could be a social system that tells us how to behave or what to expect from others, according to the way we have learned to believe that children should relate to parents. Finally, it could be a social system that categorizes and pigeonholes persons so we can always tell the good persons (those like me) from the bad ones (those who are different from me). Most of us at some time use these types of structure as cures for our hurts.

We may also use persons as cures for our hurts. A parent may find the purpose and meaning for life in children. Life has meaning only in terms of the responsibilities of a parent. "Friends" can become all-important. If that is my experience, I find myself trying to please them. I continually try to be what I think "they" want me to be. In the process there are times when I wonder who I really am. A group that I feel I belong to can be used like a balm for wounds. "I know he doesn't like me but that's because I'm white — or black — or a long-hair — or an intellectual — or Protestant — or —." "Sure the country is going to the dogs but there are lots of people who believe like I do. We are going to. . . ." I think I know who I am because I have this kind of job, live in this kind of neighborhood, drive this price-range car, drink this kind of liquor, eat these kinds of foods, like this kind of music, wear these kinds of clothes, do these kinds of things for fun. That way I identify people like me. Then I can say, "Well, if there are others like me, I can't be all bad."

Psychological Pain Is Real

The cause and the cure of inner, personal pain can be put "out there" for only so long. Sooner or later the real nature of psychological pain catches up with me and I feel it. "Life is hell!" And psychological pain is real. It is not "imaginary" or "just all in your head." It is serious. The experience of such pain may have direct and important physical consequences. Ulcers, spastic colon, colds, and other illnesses may result. Psychological pain may have direct and important consequences on our economic life. Jobs can be lost. Money may be squandered in trying to feel better. Marriages and families are broken up. Churches are changed. Murders and suicides are committed.

In fact, for most of us, this kind of pain is the most real and important pain we ever experience. Hardly anyone today in our society experiences prolonged, intractable physical pain. If we are seriously ill for a long period medication dulls the pain. Nobody is likely to hang us up by our thumbs, shock our genitalia, or otherwise impose physical torture and torment on us. The way we handle death insulates or isolates us from the stark reality of grief. Few of us have sufficient abstract ability to hurt deeply over long periods of time about the fate of the world. It is not likely that any of us will starve to death, freeze to death, or otherwise have biological survival needs denied to the point of extinction of life. Even though our welfare system may be viewed as dehumanizing, depersonalizing, and unjust, few, if any in our society, literally die from unmet biological needs.

For the great majority of us, then, the psychological pain we experience in our daily lives is the single largest factor that affects the quality of our lives. This psychological pain is produced by the accusing, condemning power of God's law in our lives. I hurt inside because I cannot meet the law's demands.

2

The Law Causes
Psychological Pain: How?

How does it really work? How does the law cause psychological pain?

Scientists, philosophers, and scholars talk about innate, given capacities of man. However, these innate capacities are not viewed as instincts, similar to animal behaviors, but rather as the capacity to perceive and infer relationships. A child, for instance, can infer syntactical rules of language. That makes it possible for him to utter grammatical sentences he has never heard before. Recent research in the way people think indicates that there are innate ways in which we organize our perceptions and symbolically represent reality.

The Christian faith, too, maintains that man has an innate capacity. The law of God is written in men's hearts. Each person is born with the fundamental, given sense of demand. It is man's nature to think of himself and his world as accused. From the beginning man senses that he stands under indictment. He attempts to respond in the only way he can know: he tries to be what he ought to be. He fails. He feels psychological pain.

The pain is primarily an emotion. The emotions we experience — including psychological pain — are caused by what we believe. Each of us possesses a complex structure of beliefs, values, and attitudes. This network forms a system that we use to explain and understand what happens. We use this system to give meaning to events, both inside and outside of us.

Two Examples

Jan, age 20, is about to graduate from college and take a job as a high school French teacher. She is very anxious about this job. She has headaches, stomach upsets, and trouble sleeping. She has a very good academic record. She spent summers in France to learn how to speak the language. She has demonstrated competence in her practice teaching. She has the contract on her desk. She can't bring herself to sign it and drop it in the mail box.

She is telling herself that she isn't really cut out to be a teacher. Maybe she ought to get a job as a waitress, or a clerk. She thinks that she might just deliberately flunk all her final exams, not graduate, and then she wouldn't have to take the job.

All of this is foolish and irrational. Everything about Jan's history indicates that she has the ability to teach. Yet she feels that she lacks the ability. Why?

She believes that to teach she must be the perfect teacher. She must always be in control of her class.

20

Everybody in the class must learn to speak perfect French in ten weeks. She believes that she must have every lesson plan fully, completely, and perfectly worked out.

In spite of her competence and academic record, on some exams she got a B instead of an A. Some lesson plans she submitted to her supervising teacher were corrected or criticized. "Obviously, I can't teach," she thinks. "I am not perfect."

It is not teaching itself that upsets Jan. It is not the unprepared student that gives Jan headaches. Rather it is what Jan *believes about* teaching that causes her psychological pain. It is Jan's beliefs that makes an unprepared student mean that *she* has failed. She does not even think that the student may not like French, or that he may not have the ability to learn it, or that he may have had a fight with his father the night before. She believes she failed. Therefore she can't teach. Therefore, she can't sign the contract.

It is what we believe about ourselves and our world that causes our emotions.

A famous psychologist is nearing the end of a brilliant and influential career. He becomes seriously depressed and talks openly of suicide. It all appears so reasonable. He believes that he can no longer produce any significant work. He belittles his previous work as imperfect, incomplete, and worthless. He says it does not meet the demands of the scientific "method" for rigor, precision, and truth. He does not see it as creative, new, adding to the body of knowledge. He laments, "What is it all for? Life no longer has any meaning. I can therefore make the rational decision to end my life."

21

He is not Christian. Yet the demand of the law is present and powerful in his life. He believes that his life has meaning only so long as it is a productive life. Productivity is measured by the standards of the scientific community. He feels that the praise and rewards the community have given him are hollow. Both he and his work are failures. He must be *more* than what he is. The voice of the law drones on, "It is not enough! It is not enough!"

The Pain of Comparison

Living under the law is a state in which we use our system of beliefs, values, and attitudes to give meaning to events. The meaning imposed on events is what causes us to feel what we feel. When the law insists that we must be different from what we are, whatever the event or situation, the beliefs that bear on that event and give it meaning will show the effect of living under the law.

The basic quality which the innate accusation of the law imposes on our system of beliefs, values, and attitudes is comparison. As we experience reality it is impossible for us to organize our perceptions in any way other than by comparative judgments. Everything is "more than . . . or less than . . . larger than . . . .smaller than. . . ." Every concept, idea, or word that we use has its opposite, its polarity. There is black and white, sweet and sour, matter and anti-matter, up and down. The effect of the law is to give us the skill of comparing, of locating everything at some point between the opposites. The primary effect of the law is evident in our capacity to measure, to count. The passion and intensity with which man measures everything, including himself, is the innate ability of the law written in every man's heart. Thorndyke's famous statement, "If anything exists, it exists in quantity. If it exists in quantity, it can be measured," sums up the effect of the law on the life of man.

When we apply our law-based measuring ability to ourselves and our relationship to the world, we feel psychological pain. However I am measuring myself I am always going to be less than I ought to be. Whether I measure myself in terms of height or weight, IQ points or behavior, morality or manners, or whatever, where I am is never enough. That will show up in the beliefs, values, and attitudes of men, even though there may be a temporary period of self-satisfaction. We have information about some of the beliefs that reflect the experience of living under the law. One major research project, *A Study of Generations,* found that there are two types of religious belief systems. One is identified as a gospel orientation and the other as a law orientation.

The law-oriented type of religious belief system shows an extreme emphasis on form and structure, on rigid and absolute thinking, on categorization and judgment of persons. The hurt and pain of living under the law produces the pessimistic, bleak attitude toward the world that is a part of this belief system. The world is a frightening and threatening place to be. There is a strong desire to force the world into rigid, secure, and dependable patterns. There is resistance to change. Religion's function is to tell what the rules are so that the appropriate measuring can be done. The concept of the self is fragile and weak. Support and satisfaction of the self is sought from outside in other persons and groups. The relationship of the individual to God is determined by his performance and achievement in measuring up to the rules. Salvation is by works.

On the other hand, the dimensions that reflect an orientation to the gospel emphasize a sense of God's involvement in human life. God's grace and care give meaning and direction to human life. The way in which God's care is evident is in the person and work of Jesus Christ. Jesus is known as one person, fully divine and fully human. He is our brother and he knows what it is to be a man. His life, death, and resurrection affirm our salvation and our justification by grace. The response of faith includes acceptance of the world as God's world. It is perceived and felt to be under God's control. That control is beneficent. Life in this world has the quality of a gift of God.

Comparing and measuring is not considered as important for one oriented to the gospel as for a law-oriented person. It has all been measured already by God. It has been measured against the standard of his grace. The comparison is that in Christ, everything is fulfilled and made perfect. This is associated with an openness to the world and to other persons.

Inside each of us is a tension between law orientation and gospel orientation. We wobble and stumble back and forth: now facing more toward the law and its demands, now by grace, facing toward the cross and its promise. These types of religious belief systems are not like boxes we get dropped into to stay put forever. They are not like rooms that we can walk into and close the door on the room left behind. It is more like being in an immense open field. All around are features of landscape. Some of them look attractive and some look frightening. But the light may shift, and what had looked bad may look a little less bad, while what had looked good may look a little dangerous. I move back and forth, now here, now there. The only sense I can make out of all of it is from the companion I have with me. He does not tug or pull in one direction with the insistent tones of a tour guide. He says, "I have been here before. I have overcome the terrors of life and death. Now they can't get you."

3

The Demand of Perfect Obedience Increases My Hurt

One powerful belief of a law-oriented person might be stated: "I must be completely obedient to the expectations of others."

This need to be obedient focuses most sharply in the family, the arena for the deepest and most intimate interpersonal relationships. The law-oriented person will tell you all of the following statements about his beliefs regarding family life:

> It is somehow unnatural to place women in positions of authority over men.
> If a child is unusual in any way, his parents should get him to be more like other children.
> A woman whose children are at all messy or rowdy has failed in her duties as a mother.
> If children are told much about sex, they are likely to go too far in experimenting with it.

A man should not be expected to have respect for a woman if they have sexual relations before they are married.

The most important qualities of a real man are determination and driving ambition.

Women who want to remove the word *obey* from the marriage service don't understand what it means to be a wife.

There is hardly anything lower than a person who does not feel a great love, gratitude, and respect for his parents.

Some equality in marriage is a good thing, but by and large the husband ought to have the main say-so in family matters.

The facts on crime and sexual immorality show that we will have to crack down harder on young people if we are going to save our moral standards.

If a child is allowed to talk back to his parents, he will lose respect for them.

You may object, "But there is a way that God wants us to live in the family. God has set it up for the husband to be the head of the family. Children are supposed to be obedient. After all, there is the Fourth Commandment." True, there is a Fourth Commandment. True, Scripture calls the husband the head of the wife and family. But how? In love as Christ loved. That is different from demanding obedience.

Would you go on to say, "If a person — husband, wife, or child — doesn't obey and do what is expected, then he is no good, a failure, and deserves to be damned"? "No, of course not," you say. The following instances describe people who felt they were not obedient and who experienced consequences of that feeling in their lives.

**A man should not be expected to have respect
for a woman if they have sexual relations
before they are married.**

Ruth fell in love and became engaged to Fred during
her college years. After becoming engaged she had
sexual intercourse with Fred on several occasions. This
was her first sexual experience. Two months before the
wedding Fred broke the engagement and refused to
marry Ruth. For about six months Ruth was rather
depressed, but then she met Harold. Three months
later Harold and Ruth married.

Five years later Ruth had a two-year-old daughter,
an unsatisfactory sex life (she never experienced an
orgasm), and serious depression. She hated her house
and spent most of her time visiting her mother and
sisters who lived nearby. She was on the verge of
divorcing Harold because she was convinced she had a
bad marriage.

Ruth had never told Harold about Fred. She couldn't.
She believed that if she did Harold could not love her.
She did not meet the standard she believed was expected of her — to be virginal at the time of marriage.
As a result her life had become hell, lived under a
constant sense of accusation. She was not what she
ought to be. She needed to be something different.

After coming to understand that her own self-blame
and self-judgment were making her feel depressed and
unhappy with her marriage, Ruth was able to tell
Harold about her affair with Fred. Fortunately, in this
case, Harold could accept Ruth's past without blaming
her. They worked it out and now, two years later, Ruth
has an infant son, a fully satisfactory sex life, and hap-
pily cares for her children and house.

**If a child is unusual in any way, his parents
should get him to be more like other children.**

Linnea is hurting. She does not sleep well. She is
tired all the time. Periodically she blows up. There is a
huge scene and she storms out of the house threatening never to return. She is 38, bright, reasonably attractive, and highly talented artistically. She is married
to John, a college professor. She says, "My boys (ages
11 and 8) are not like other boys. The oldest, Kevin,
doesn't play with other kids at all. He can't get along
with anyone. The youngest, Kent, is very pushy and
throws tantrums whenever he doesn't get his way.
John isn't strong with them at all. He never disciplines
or controls them. He never gets angry. He is always
calm and tries to talk things out. It just infuriates me.
I wish he would just tell me what to do. If only he
would get mad at me — just once show some feeling.
Sometimes I dream about — about being forced —
raped."

Linnea believes there is just one way for her sons,
her husband, and herself to be. Obviously they are not
the way they should be. It turns out that Linnea is
constantly nagging, criticizing, and pushing her sons
and her husband to be and do what she thinks they
ought to be. Neither they nor she ever succeed. She
has a rich fantasy life in which she is happy, the perfect
wife and mother. Daydreaming about this fantasy
world occupies much of her time.

For Linnea her need to be obedient and her knowledge that she is not obedient leads her to seek an
authority that will control and direct her. She looks to
her husband to be that authority. She pleads with John
to be a strong, dominant leader. But just let him try!

Then comes the explosion! Whenever John tries to give advice and assert some control in the family, Linnea feels it is a judgment. "Well, honey, why don't you do . . ." translates for Linnea, "You are not doing what you should be doing. You are a bad wife. You are a failure as a mother." That hurts. Linnea explodes. This system has Linnea expecting, even inviting, punishment. Punishment is the only response that would make sense to Linnea. After all, that is what she has coming. The only time that Linnea has a positive experience is when she has exploded and left home in anger. She drives around for a few hours, envisioning herself alone, friendless, unloved, promiscuous, and abused, an outcast on Skid Row. For a moment, by this fantasy, she satisfies the guilt of not being what she ought to be. Then she can return, kiss and make up, and make love sweetly and tenderly.

God is a God of order, not of chaos. There is a structure and a system, an order, for family life that God has ordained. The law-oriented person sees that. However, he sees the system God has ordained *only* as a demand to be obeyed. He sees nothing else. That is why the following statements are a part of the law-oriented view of family life:

> If a child is unusual in any way, his parents should get him to be more like other children.
>
> If children are told much about sex, they are likely to go too far in experimenting with it.
>
> A woman whose children are at all messy or rowdy has failed in her duties as a mother.
>
> There is hardly anything lower than a person who does not feel a great love, gratitude, and respect for his parents.

A man should not be expected to have respect for a woman if they have sexual relations before they are married.

The most important qualities of a real man are determination and driving ambition.

These attitudes show the need for obedience to standards of family life, reliance on conformity to what others expect, and the conviction that if you don't measure up, you have failed.

The most important qualities of a real man are determination and driving ambition.

The crippling effects of the sense of failure to be obedient is clear in Ron's life. Ron is 28 years old. He works as a lab technician. Ron is not married. He was engaged to a young woman whom he dearly loved. The day before the wedding Ron backed out. He couldn't go through with it even though he loved his fiancee. It was because of that love that he believed he could not marry. He was not good enough. For two years after the breakup Ron lived with remorse, sadness, and despair. Then he sought help.

It turned out that Ron had a very capable, ambitious father. Ron was his firstborn son. The father insisted that Ron become an engineer as he was. There was heavy emphasis on grades, achievement, and ambition. The early pattern was that Ron's report card would have five A's and one B. The father would rage at Ron, "What's wrong with you? You dummy! You got this B. You're stupid! You're not trying hard enough!" Soon Ron's grades were all C's or less. He was expelled from an exclusive boys' college-preparatory school for as-

32

saulting the English teacher. When Ron was 17, the father committed suicide.

By the time Ron came to my office, he had piled up over 100 incompletes at the local university. His pattern was to enroll each quarter, faithfully attend all classes, do his studying assiduously — until the mid-quarter test. When that came up, Ron would thoroughly prepare, but the day of the test, he just could not go. He absolutely believed he would fail, so he could not take the test. He stayed home and curled up in bed. After the mid-quarter he no longer attended classes and did not show up for the finals. Thus he got "Incompletes" for every class. The next quarter he would say, "I will try harder. It will be different this time."

Ron's IQ measured in the very superior range. He had the ability to complete college, even graduate school. He believed that he was worthless unless he finished college and got the degree, the same one as his father. He had not completed college. Therefore, he was worthless. He loved his fiancee. Therefore he could not marry her. If he did, she would be saddled with a worthless, ambitionless failure. He could not do that to her.

It took time, but after Ron understood his need for obedience and his sense of failure, he was able to get hold of the belief that his personal value and worth did not depend on the level of his obedience. He returned to school. This time he did what he wanted — studied business and economics rather than engineering. He completed his work, obtained the degree, and got a job he was pleased with. The last word I heard from him was an invitation to his wedding.

33

**If children are told much about sex, they are
likely to go too far in experimenting with it.**

Tom is 21, tall, handsome, with black, curly hair, a
a luxuriant mustache, and very well built. He looks like
a young Paul Newman. He is in a construction trade
apprenticeship program. His problem is that he has
never been able to complete coitus. He has tried since
age 16. He has never managed to maintain an erection.
This has convinced him that he is not a real man. He
attempted homosexual relations out of the belief that
if he couldn't succeed with a woman, he must be a
"queer." That did not work for Tom. He tried being
an "actor" in a pornographic film. That did not work
either in spite of hours of skilled effort by several
sexually experienced females.

At the time he came for help, Tom's sexual inadequacy had become the focus of his entire life. He was
contemplating suicide as the only way to escape the
pain of his impotency. He surely could not think of
marriage. He was about to be dropped from his apprenticeship training because he could not concentrate
on his work.

Tom's parents were post-World War II displaced
persons. After emigration to America they both worked
hard, lived frugally, and built a secure life economi-
cally. There was no talk about sex at all, except when
Tom's father got drunk. Then he would tell Tom that
he would never be a man until he had intercourse. He
would belittle women, tease Tom about the size of his
penis, and use gross and vulgar language in describing
his own sexual exploits.

When Tom made his first attempt at coitus and
failed, he believed he was a failure as a man. He was

34

convinced that he was not measuring up to the standard by which he judged himself, a standard that insisted he perform adequately. His actions, reprehensible as they may be, were a desperate attempt to find a way, any way, in which he could meet the demand he felt to be obedient to what was expected of him.

The experience of the four persons shows what can happen when the demand that we must measure up is felt in every area of life. The belief that we must be perfectly obedient, completely adequate, and totally competent is actually the notion that we must be divine rather than human. That is clearly a ridiculous and impossible demand. Yet it is exactly what the law says, "Be therefore perfect even as your father in heaven is perfect." The law-oriented person hears only that statement. He hears nothing else. The result is a painful life.

The church is not the chief propagandist for the demand of the law. The society, the culture around us, relentlessly dins into our ears that we must be obedient. The law is the way God relates to the world outside of the church. The law is the natural religion of men. That is why homes, schools, magazines, movies, advertisements, television, and every other means of communication constantly tell us that we must measure up, be obedient to what is expected.

Take the demand that we must smell good as an example. TV commercials say you will fail in love, fail in business, fail in sports, in school, fail everywhere unless you use brand X deodorant under your arms, brand Y on your face, and brand Z on your genitals. There is no more clear expression of cultural propagandizing for the law than that poor TV policeman directing traffic on a hot summer day. When he raises his arms and discovers his "wetness" in the armpits, his expression of dismay and embarrassment sums up the effect of the law. He is caught! He is not what he ought to be—dry under the arms.

Multiply that kind of message by the thousands, covering every aspect of life, and you will get some idea of the subtlety and pervasiveness of the cultural commitment to the law. It is not only evident in rather crude, earthy areas like body odor, but also in more positive, desirable areas. Millions of American mothers are convinced that unless they love their children perfectly, all of the time, awake and sleeping, they will shatter their kids' psyches forever. Fathers believe that if they are not "buddies" to their children, they have failed miserably.

This belief has been called the "spun glass theory of the mind." It has become particularly virulent since the days of Sigmund Freud and his heavy emphasis on traumatic childhood events as the trigger for repression of feelings. The result is that many of the women any psychotherapist sees are paralyzed by the belief that they have not obeyed the demand to be perfectly loving mothers. They have taken all of the 10-question tests in women's magazines to find out if they are good mothers. They fail every one. They are not good mothers. They become anxious, worried, depressed. They wind up in the therapist's office. There they learn that they will be good mothers if only they measure up to their therapist's idea as to what a good mother is. The law in men's hearts wins again.

Young people today emphasize honesty and openness—on being non-phony. A young woman whom I saw was completely crushed while planning an anti-war rally. One of her coworkers told her she was a phony, a fraud. He said that her involvement in the anti-war movement was a "head trip." That is one of the worst sins you can commit when you are young and aware of the human-potential movements. The young woman felt guilty, inadequate, self-doubting, and self-blaming. She believed and felt that she was disobedient.

The effect of the law in men's hearts is not limited to disobedience to the Ten Commandments. If we think only of the Commandments we will see only a small portion of the impact that the law truly has. What the law sets up rather is a system. The system is simply our habit of measuring and evaluating ourselves in terms of obedience-disobedience. The standard by which we examine our level of obedience-disobedience can be anything.

In a congregation, heeding the scriptural counsel that all things be done decently and in order, a procedure for getting people from their seats to the communion rail is set up by the worship committee. A plan is devised that says where each group stands while waiting, how many are to be in each group, which direction people turn when leaving the communion rail, and which aisle is used to return to the seats. The bulletin carefully explains the procedures. Ushers are strategically placed to direct traffic.

Everything works smoothly. People are following the plan. Ushers graciously channel the flow. They assist elderly people up the chancel steps. The congregation watches and learns what is expected of them. Time is saved and the service is completed five minutes earlier than usual.

Watch what happens when a visitor or a member makes a mistake and turns the "wrong way." You can visibly see the hesitation, the awful realization, the instant blush, the confusion, the jerky movement of arms and legs trying to cover up. Like our TV policeman, you are *caught!* You have not done what others expected. The shame, guilt, and embarrassment that flood you effectively destroy any sense of forgiveness that may have come to you in the sacrament. The law wins again! You stand accused!

The accusation that you have failed to be obedient does not depend on the specific content of the demand. The constant accusation leads to the feeling that you must try even harder to obey perfectly. The result is an impossible demand that increases your hurt.

4

I Hurt Because
I Fear Change

If I live under the constant demand to be obedient to the expectations of others, I can feel good about myself only if I can prove to myself that I am living up to their expectations. I find the demand impossible. The more I try to be perfectly obedient, the less sure I become of my performance. My hurt increases with my failures to meet the impossible demand of perfect obedience.

My hurt increases even more if I am afraid that the rules established by people and outside forces may change. This means that the rules, the standards by which everything is measured, must remain stable. It is frustrating to play a game with somebody who makes up new rules on the spot. I used to play Monopoly at about age 10. There were two people I soon learned not to play with. They seemed always to want to change the rules. Whenever they did, I could never win.

The law-oriented person is in the same position. He is striving hard to be obedient. His life is built on the rules. If those rules change or shift, everything goes smash. There is no way he can feel he is obedient any more. Therefore he wants to keep the rules the same as they have always been. He is highly resistant to any changes. Not every person who rejects changes is necessarily a law-oriented person. Changes may be judged to be unwise, ineffective, or potentially destructive. Changes can be resisted on rational grounds. The law-oriented person, however, rejects the very concept of change, not only specific changes.

A law-oriented person is likely to tell you about his fears of change immediately after he tells you his beliefs about family life. He will say *all* of the following statements:

> If I were to follow my deepest concern, I would concentrate on trying to preserve the very best of a long tradition. This seems to me to be a primary need today.
>
> My first reaction when I think of the future is to be aware of its dangers.
>
> We Christians have to exercise caution when we act in the local community, because it is so easy for those outside the church to misinterpret what we are trying to do.
>
> When you are young, you can afford to be an enthusiastic supporter of reform and change, but as you grow older, you learn that it is wiser to be cautious about making changes.
>
> The best way to improve world conditions is for each man to take care of his own corner of the vineyard.
>
> The world is a pretty good place. We really don't need all this concern about change.
>
> The future is in God's hands. I will await what he sends and accept what comes as his will for me

He is telling you clearly that he wants to keep things the way they are. He is also telling you that he fears what other people think about what he does. They might not like it so you really have to be cautious about what you do. The future is frightening to him. He wants to concentrate on his own life. He will live it by the rules in his own place. He does not want other people to interfere. He will leave them alone, too, as long as the rules stay the same.

If I were to follow my deepest concern,
I would concentrate on trying to preserve
the very best of a long tradition.
This seems to me to be a primary need today.

Amanda had taught art at the same women's college for 45 years. She had studied art in Paris in the 1920s. There she adopted the philosophy and style of the French Impressionists. When she retired at age 70 she was still alert, active, and energetic. She had carefully laid plans to open an art gallery upon her retirement. Several younger women, many of them former students, had agreed to go in with her. The gallery opened the day after Amanda's retirement with a very pleasant tea. A cordial, warm group of friends filled the place. They admired a collection of Amanda's works, hung to open the gallery. Amanda was radiantly happy. She had looked forward eagerly to the years of retirement.

Within three months Amanda appeared in my office. She could not sleep. Her appetite was gone. She sat in the gallery and cried. She flew into uncontrolled rage at meetings of the group of women running the gallery. She was highly critical of the choice of paintings and artists to be displayed. She fussed about schedules of

41

working times, finances, advertising. She was rude to visitors in the gallery. All of this deeply puzzled her. She said, "I have turned into a grade-A bitch. I never used to be this way! What has happened to me?"

What had happened? The rules had changed for Amanda. She no longer had the protected position of power—her classroom—to preserve the tradition of Impressionism. The other women wanted to include works of other styles in the gallery. Some even criticized Impressionism as out of date. Potential customers liked art that Amanda felt they should not like. Amanda responded with anger and harsh criticism of their tastes. The standards by which she had measured her life and her self were threatened and challenged by her new experience. Living under the demand of the law had been fairly comfortable for 45 years. She had externalized the cure by her heavy and intense identification with the beliefs, values, and life style of the left bank of Paris in the '20s. When that no longer worked, Amanda's response was anger, depression, and confusion. She never managed a second adjustment to the law. She died three years later, bitter and isolated to the end.

My first reaction when I think of the future is to be aware of its dangers.

For the last year George had been very angry and harsh with his six children and his wife. He drank more heavily than he ever had before. He neglected the lawn and garden at his suburban hobby farm. After 20 years of payments and loving care, his 15 acres were finally his. Now his hobby farm seemed like a prison. His annual fishing and hunting trips were disasters. He caught little. He missed shots. He disagreed bitterly with his companions. The last two days of duck hunting he stayed in the cabin, drunk.

George had been a model employee for 22 years in the shipping department of a large firm. Now his supervisor had been replaced by a younger man. The job rules had been changed. New work procedures were required by computerization of the inventory. George's oldest child, his son, had enlisted. He was in Vietnam. His oldest daughter was beginning to date.

Whereas George had been happy, outgoing, and friendly, now he was gloomy, pessimistic, and irritable. He thought only of problems. How could he work under the new situation? Would his son return? Would his daughter marry well? How could he keep his farm with taxes doubling every year? How could he stop the encroachment of suburban development?

George had everything he had dreamed of for a lifetime—a loving wife, children, a secure job, his own place free and clear. It did not make any difference. In fact, he felt worse when he looked at the fruits of his labor. He thought, "How can I feel so bad when I have all of this? Something is really wrong with me!"

George had kept the law as he knew it. It said to him, "Do this and you will get that." George did it and he got it. But now how could he keep it? The future was ominous and foreboding. It was filled with threats. George had no responses available to meet the threats that he felt other than more hard work, more striving, more keeping the rules. So he clamped down hard on his wife and children. He made heavy demands of his friends. He tried hard to keep everything the way it had been. He did not want anything to change.

But George's solution does not work. The world changes around us. Children grow up. Bosses retire and new bosses change the rules. Friends die or move away. Taxes go up. Dollars buy less. Companies merge with others or some go out of business. A sense of security built on external factors like home, friends, or a job is peculiarly vulnerable to the inevitable process of change. No matter how hard George tried, he could not keep his world intact, frozen into a state of happiness. He became frustrated, angry, and depressed all at once. Everything that had once been so important to George now became a source of irritation. He kept going back to the well, but now it was dry.

This illustrates the inevitable frustration and pain of living under the law. It tells me that I must be different. I try hard. I depend on the rules to tell me what I should really work at. For a time I can feel fairly good, but then the rules begin to shift under my feet. Things change. No matter how hard I try by the old rules, it will not work. The future looks grim.

Caution! Go Slow!

Two of the statements that characterize the law-oriented person stress caution about making any changes. Making any changes is a fearsome thing. Therefore, go slow. Be very sure of your ground. Test out any change first before you make the move.

Carl served as elder in a suburban parish. A new pastor was encouraging greater community involvement and more aggressive evangelism. At the same time Carl was contemplating buying a drugstore of his own after 20 years as pharmacist at the same store.

Carl found it increasingly difficult to sleep. His mind went round and round about his responsibility as elder and his chance to go into business. He sat up late and woke up early. He tried to figure out every possibility. Most of them were bad. As he dispensed tranquilizers, he began to tell himself that he needed them. He did not want them, but he knew something had to give.

Rather than admit his problem to his physician, Carl began to take a mild tranquilizer on his own. He immediately began to fret about himself as well as his pastor and business opportunity. Now he knew he had changed. He began to literally measure his self-worth in terms of the amount of medication he used each day. If he used more, it was a bad day and he was a bad person. If he used less, he was good and it was a good day. If a prescription came in for a smaller dosage than he was taking, he knew immediately that he was worse than that person. His sleeping problem became more serious. Larger doses and major tranquilizers did not help.

When Carl finally came for help, he was in bad shape. As he understood his fears of change, his sense of inadequacy, and his habit of catastrophizing (seeing all the worst possible outcomes), Carl was able to work through the sense of the demand of the law. First, he stopped measuring himself by the amount of medications. Then he dropped tranquilizers. He risked talking to his pastor. He risked going into business. Both situations worked out well for Carl. He is no longer paralyzed by the prospects of change.

When a man measures himself by how well he conforms to the rules, a dependable world is a vital necessity. If the world and its rules change, a man literally doesn't know who he is anymore. All of his efforts of the past feel worthless. If he accepts new rules, he has to admit either that he was wrong or foolish before. Both alternatives are painful. That is why many Roman Catholics found it difficult to accept changes following the Second Vatican Council. Protestants, too, frequently express the sentiment, "We will stay with the old ways." Change, in itself, is not necessarily good. But neither is the familiar past necessarily good. The man living under the law has a weak critical ability. He finds it difficult to examine proposed changes or to risk them. He finds it difficult to critically evaluate the past. There is too much at stake in preserving the measuring devices, whatever they may be, by which he is defending himself against the accusation of the law.

There may be valid reasons for deciding that a given change is neither wise nor necessary. Each man must make his own evaluation. The law-oriented person, however, has a knee-jerk reaction against any change. Within the church it is likely that the most vehement, persistent, and irrational opposition to change is linked to a law orientation. This does not mean that a given individual opposing changes is law-oriented. Nor does it mean that a person favoring change is necessarily gospel-oriented. It does mean that a person who relies on external structures, customs, and rules to measure oneself and others, will have a strong resistance to change and with it a rather painful life.

Let us also examine the last three statements that show the resistance to change among law-oriented persons. "The future is in God's hands. I will await what he sends and accept what comes as his will for me." "The world as it is is a pretty good place. We really don't need all this concern about change." "The best way to improve world conditions is for each man to take care of his own corner of the vineyard." The neat thing about the first is that the law-oriented person can sound pious. At the same time he is not required to do anything at all. "Leave it in God's hands. I will go about my business. I will take care of me and mine. You do the same and we will all be happy. Nothing will change. Nothing needs to change because this is a pretty good world as it is." What looks like piety is in reality passive resistance to anything new.

After four years of marriage and two children Lois was divorced. She moved back in with her parents. She occupied the same room in which she had been born. She went to work. For 28 years Lois rode the same bus morning and evening. She went to the same department store office five days a week. She did the same task—accounts payable—gradually rising to a supervisory position. Every Sunday she went to the same church where she had been baptized and confirmed and married. She confidently expected to be buried from there also. She made the same pledge every year and faithfully kept it.

Her children grew up, found jobs, but remained in the home. There were some problems, but they were remote. They had to do with other people. Lois, her parents, and her children could not stand Jews, blacks, lazy poor people, or Communists. Since there were no such people around them, they simply clucked about such crazy, foolish people and their wicked ways, reassuring themselves in family devotions that God was in charge.

Then all hell broke loose into Lois' life. One morning

she came to work and found a new boss. The department store had been purchased by a large eastern firm. They had sent out a new manager. He had instructions to install new business methods utilizing computers. He was to change the image of the store to a swinging, modern, chic, high-fashion establishment. He hired new people. Some of them were black. Some were young. He was Jewish.

Within two months Lois was a wreck. She quit or was fired. She stayed home in her room. She was angry with her children, her aged parents, her God. She did not go to church. She typed long, bitter, incoherent letters to nobody in particular. She burst into violent tirades against wickedness and evil in the world. When her unemployment compensation ran out, her son persuaded her to seek help. It was too late. She is still hospitalized. She curses God for failing her. She had kept her part of the bargain. She tended her vineyard. God did not keep his word. He changed the rules on her.

Knowing only the law meant that Lois expected her faithful performance to force God to keep everything in her life stable and sure. When it didn't work that way, Lois reacted violently. Her life is now hell. She is estranged from God and from other people. Her reaction may be more extreme than most. Nevertheless, when to live is to measure and then when God seemingly does not measure up, life gets quite painful.

All that is left is to hope for death. Death is the final demand of the law. It makes mockery of the attempts to freeze the law into stable rules. It may happen that life works out quite well and there have not been too many changes. It may even be that there has not been too much pain. By all of the procedures of obedience and resistance to change, I may have succeeded in taming the law, cutting it down to manageable size. The futility of a lifetime of domesticating the radical demands of the law is evident in the final event— death. Things will change then.

The need to be obedient and the consequent desire for stability in life are the two most powerful factors in a law orientation. The accusing demand, "You must be different from what you are," brings about the need for obedience. This need produces resistance to change. The inherent frustration and pain of such a life is compelled by the human situation. The law cannot be kept. Every attempt to locate both law and obedience to it in structures outside of the individual fails. No system of behaviors, roles, expectations, relationships, or anything else can deliver what is hoped for— internal peace.

5

I Feel Accused
and Accuse Others

Living under the law means to feel constantly accused. To meet the accusation life becomes entirely a matter of measured obedience. The degree of obedience-disobedience may be measured with any kind or type of yardstick.

Peter measured his life in terms of physical contact with his girl friend of many years. Every time he thought of holding her hand or putting his arm around her, he was overwhelmed by the fear of rejection. His whole life was at stake. He could not afford to fail. Thus he withdrew each time he thought of it. He tried to avoid failure and consequently failed. She married somebody who showed some interest in her.

At age 14 Joan measured her life in terms of her ability to steal better than her friends.

Jean's measure was production of children. She was diabetic. She was convinced she would be dead by age 40. Having children became the central fact of her life. She appeared in my office two years after her marriage complaining of compulsive eating contrary to her diabetic diet. She had not gotten pregnant in the normal way. If she got fat she would at least look pregnant.

For Alan, a brilliant law student, the obedience-disobedience standard was his success in taking the easy way. He became very upset when he found he had to study more in his final year of law school.

Genevieve almost flunked out of graduate school rather than study. To prepare like her fellow students would be to admit that she did not measure up to her standards.

And so it goes. For all who evaluate their life and themselves by the extent to which they measure up, the result is failure and pain. What is important is *not* what is used as the measure. The crucial factor is the process of measurement. Living only under the law imposes that process as a continuous, constant activity. There is no relief. Never. There are only delusional moments of temporary satisfaction with "a job well done." Sooner or later the insistent voice of the law, "It is not enough!" breaks through the defenses to shatter the illusion of satisfaction of the demand.

You Can't Win

Persons living under the law must necessarily have what psychologists have called a "weak ego." Laymen may term the more obvious result lack of self-confidence or feelings of inferiority. Another way to view the consequences of living only under the law is to use the language of self-acceptance, self-fulfillment, or

52

self-realization. Whatever those terms may mean, there is no way for a man living under the demand of the law to feel good about himself.

The subtle trap which the law sets up to defeat every attempt of man to satisfy its demand is evident in the lives of persons who attempt the prescription of the self-realization, self-fulfillment school. To be a self-accepting, self-realized person becomes another form of demand. How do I ever know if I am self-accepting enough? As long as there is a goal, no matter what the specific content of that goal may be, the self-conscious nature of personhood dictates that measurement and evaluation will occur. Failure inevitably follows. "It is not enough!" There just is no way for a person to escape that accusation from within his own resources.

The Search for Others Like Me

One way to try to escape is to find other persons like ourselves. It does not really matter which dimensions are used to identify groups of persons like myself. Anything will do. Nor does it matter what I call this habit of grouping — clubbiness, social roles, or ethnicity. The curious fact is that even anarchists and nihilists have conventions.

However, try as I will, as long as I live only under the law, I cannot do anything to anybody else that I cannot do to myself. Measuring and evaluating my life and my self is my constant habit. Thus measuring and evaluating others is also my constant habit. *What* I use to measure by is not nearly as important as the *act* of measurement itself. When I use the process of measurement and evaluation to identify groups of persons like me, two things happen.

First, I find that, indeed, there are other persons similar to myself. There are others who are fathers, or like detective stories, or have blue eyes, or get a kick out of the beauty of snowflakes or the "rush" of heroin. There are others who are successes or failures. There are others who beat their children or write sonnets.

There are even others who are hermits or recluses. There are others who believe that they should accept other people just as they are.

But — how good a father? How pure and undefiled a hermit? How truly and honestly accepting of others? How cruel in beating children — less or more than me? How blue the eyes? How humane and unprejudicial? How skilled a scientist or tiddly-winks player? How great a degree of ESP? Whatever the similarity, I do the same thing to the other person that I do to myself: I locate him along the standard. I measure him. I measure me.

The result is that I have a rather clear picture (not necessarily an accurate one) of the relative position of other persons and myself. That position can be along any kind or type of yardstick. The subject or content of the comparison is not as significant as the fact of the comparative judgment.

Generally we are not necessarily aware of all the comparative judgments we have available to fix our self in relation to other people. However, if pressed, most of us are able to tell where we are in relation to other people along measurements we may never have consciously thought of before. The total of all such comparative judgments about myself and others is a large part of my self-concept and self-image.

This measurement of myself and others is a major factor in determining the degree of attraction or liking/disliking I have for other people. For most of us, if not for all, the greater the similarity between myself and others, the greater the degree of attraction. The greater the perceived dissimilarity, the greater the distance we wish to keep.

The law-oriented person has a very powerful interest in this whole process of self-and-other measurement. The law is always accusing him. He tries to meet that accusation by finding others like him. A group is created. That group becomes his in-group. Of necessity, then, persons who do not fit in that group become the out-group. This is the second consequence of the measurement process. Both in-group and out-group are necessary for defense against the accusation of the law.

The in-group serves the function of meeting the accusation of the law with the claim, "Well, I'm not so bad. See! There are other people like me." The out-group supports the claim, "I'm not so bad! See! There are others worse than I." Members of either group who are "better" than I permit the plea, "Now look, don't expect so much of me. After all, I'm not as good or able as those people. Be realistic! I'm doing the best I can."

Alienation and Prejudice

The importance of self-and-other measurement to the law-oriented person is supported by the findings of

A Study of Generations. Every measure of discrimination, prejudice, and desire to keep social distance from others that was revealed by the pattern of responses is found in the factor of law orientation. This means that the heaviest dependence on locating myself in relation to others is characteristic of a life lived only under the law.

It is somewhat like being an insect. The constant demand of the law mushes me into a soft, quivering, mass of jelly. I need something to give some shape and firmness to me. I look outside of myself to groups, structures, rigid practices, and expectations of various kinds. I build an external skeleton for myself, like the insect's hard shell that holds his soft insides together.

The pain of living only under the law is generated by the inevitable failure of any external group or structure to deliver the goods. The very things I am looking for help intensify the problem. The more sharply and harshly I measure other people, the more sharply and harshly I measure myself. I cannot do anything to anybody else without already doing it to myself, either loving or hating. Alienation from self and from others is the end result of the law-induced process of measurement.

Alienation and prejudice are certainly regarded by many as two of the most important factors in contemporary life. Alienation is used to describe the central quality of modern life. There are "alienated" youth. There are "alienated" oldsters. There are "alienated" blacks and Indians. There are "alienated" males. There are "alienated" females. "Alienated" is used to describe individuals, groups, movements, and subcultures. This is called an "age of alienation."

Prejudice is regarded as the most troublesome evil barring the way to the realization of a just and humane society. Massive social, political, religious, and economic efforts have been made to understand and eradicate prejudice. They have failed. We are beginning to be a bit more sophisticated about prejudice. We now know that prejudice is not limited to the stereotyped "redneck" of Mississippi who abuses and even lynches black people. Prejudice is not limited to WASP types. There is anti-Semitism in Communist Russia. There is mass slaughter of Hindus by Moslems, and Moslems by Hindus. There is the thoughtless slaughter of "gooks" by American GIs. Hundreds of thousands die in new African nations when one tribe begins genocide against another.

Where is the utopia promised by the optimism of the 19th century? Where is the rational society of the social engineers? Students today have gained much attention for their efforts to build an alternative culture based on a collectivist, personal relations approach. There have been many experiments in communes, group living, cooperatives of various kinds. After several years of experience we find the half-life of such ventures to be about three to four months. The more perceptive students are very upset that even in their immediately personal lives it has proven impossible (thus far) to live out the ideal of a just and humane society.

I suggest that the inability to find a way to realize the ideal of a non-alienated, non-prejudiced social structure is caused by the subtle but powerful effect of living only under the demand of the law. It is the innate measurement process set up in the hearts of all men by the presence of the law that issues in the defeat of every attempt of men to build a just and humane society. There can be no open society as long as the accusation of the law closes the hearts of individuals.

A Study of Generations shows that prejudicial and judgmental attitudes toward other persons is a part of a law-oriented life. It also demonstrates that prejudice is generalized. Persons are not prejudiced against Jews only and accepting of blacks, Communists, drug addicts, or members of the John Birch Society. If a person is prejudiced, that is, makes a sharp, clear, and negative comparison between the group he belongs to and other groups of persons, he is prejudiced against a broad band of groups or types of persons.

In *A Study of Generations* law orientation is a relatively unsophisticated factor. It is more characteristic of persons with a lower level of education. Many of the items are of the kind that would not be agreed to by a moderately bright college graduate who reads the popular news magazines, has a few sociological paperbacks on his bookshelves (left over from his college days), and buys Paul Klee prints for his living room.

However, if the effects of living only under the law are as described here, we would expect that persons sophisticated enough to avoid obvious and gross statements that are socially unpopular in today's world would still show the effects of life under the law. This would mean that we expect to find intact the basic measurement process of self and others. The only thing that would be different is the standard or rule used to evaluate self and others.

This is borne out in the observation that persons

showing little prejudice or intolerance toward racial or social groups are quite intolerant of persons who do. During some campus disturbances a patient with some minor physical complaints came to a physician. During the course of the conversation the patient remarked that he wished the police would club hell out of all those long-haired radical communist students. The physician immediately kicked the man out of his office, refusing to treat him. Who is showing a greater amount of prejudice and intolerance?

The prejudices of the left are just as violent as the prejudices of the right. The wholesale rejection of persons and groups by the humanistic intelligentsia is equally as severe as that of the superstitious masses. Possibly the extreme tragedy inherent in the frustration of living only under the law is expressed in the act of Richard Wishnetsky. On the morning of February 12, 1966, he murdered Rabbi Morris Adler in full view of the congregation of Sharey Zedek synagogue of Detroit. He killed Rabbi Adler as a protest against the phoniness and hypocrisy of the world.

Before the murder Wishnetsky addressed the congregation. The tape recorder set up to record the rabbi's Bar Mitzvah sermon caught Wishnetsky's words also.

> This congregation is a travesty and an abomination. It has made a mockery by its phoniness and hypocrisy of the beauty and spirit of Judaism. . . . It is composed of men, women, and children who are for nothing except their vain and egotistical selves. With this act I protest a humanly horrifying and hence unacceptable solution.

In a note written the day before the killing Wishnetsky gives a clear statement of his motives and the meaning, to him, of his deed.

> My distorted, disoriented voice, either barely uttered or tremendously violent, gives you a slight horrifying glimpse into the dehumanized future that awaits you and your unfortunate children, who will be healthy, comfortable, and secure beyond your fondest dreams and just as diseased. Since I feel that I am no longer able to make any significant creative contributions, I shall make a destructive one. What happened in Sharey Zedek happens only once in a lifetime. . . . Suffer in your frozen hells of apathy, boil in the self-hate of outraged impotence. Listen to my voice, you deaf ones. Listen to how sick, sad, lonely, and forlorn it is.

Wishnetsky measured himself. He was not adequate. The law made it clear. His life, he, himself — "It is not enough!" He measured others. They were inadequate, too. Diseased. Phony. Hypocrites. "Just as I am," he said. He killed.

In short, what passes for man's irrationality, man's inhumanity to man, wherever and however it appears, under whatever guise or rationale, is the inevitable consequence of experiencing only life under the law. It has ever been thus. It will ever be thus, so long as men live knowing and hearing only "It is not enough!" The law written in men's hearts compels him to seek his being in self-negation. He must seek to be what he is not — perfect — and not to be what he is — sinful. Either way, his being is denied and canceled. What he does to himself he must do to others. This is the source of our inability to build community without excluding those who are different. What a person must judge and reject about himself, he must judge and reject in others. Hence the importance of the prayer of the unknown Edinburgh weaver, "God, help me always to keep a good opinion of myself." It is only what we can accept about ourselves that we can accept in others.

Some of the measurements and evaluations that a law orientation applies to others are reflected in the results of *A Study of Generations*. One of the dimensions of a law-oriented misbelief system contains all of the following statements:

> Most people who live in poverty could do something about it if they really wanted to.
>
> Poor people would be better off if they took advantage of the opportunities available to them rather than spending so much time protesting.
>
> Negroes could solve many of their own problems if they would not be so irresponsible and carefree about life.
>
> Jews always like to be at the head of things.
>
> Jews are more willing than others to use shady practices to get what they want.
>
> Jews have a lot of irritating faults.
>
> Jews don't care what happens to anyone but their own kind.
>
> The trouble with Jewish businessmen is that they are so shrewd and tricky that other people don't have a fair chance in competition.
>
> No punishment is too severe for those guilty of sex killings.
>
> Although there is no essential difference between blacks and whites, it is preferable for them not to mingle socially.

Conscientious objectors should be treated as traitors to their country.

(Saying "I disagree") Jews are just as honest as other businessmen.

(Saying, "I disagree") I have no objection to Negroes and whites dating each other.

Jews are more loyal to Israel than to America.

People (white or black) have a right to keep others out of their neighborhood if they want to, and this right should be respected.

These statements reflect at least part of the law-oriented rejection of others. They deal with poor people, Negroes, and Jews and other groups that don't follow the rules. There are two basic elements in each statement: first, a group is identified (poor people, sex offenders, Jews, etc.); second, the identified group is described as rule breakers. "They" are evaluated as evil. "They" are evil because "they" are not doing or being what "they" ought to be doing or being. Therefore they can legitimately and reasonably be rejected.

The other two measures found in *A Study of Generations* that show rejecting attitudes as a part of a law orientation simply rank 20 stereotyped groups of persons (Communists, alcoholics, whites, etc.) in terms of how distant or how close "they" are permitted to come. Persons who fit in some groups can be admitted close enough for me to marry one of them, i.e., non-Lutheran Protestants. Persons fitting in other groups need to be kept at such a distance that I don't even want them to be allowed in my country, i.e., Communists or homosexuals. Here we meet the effects of a law orientation on societies. Indeed, the existence of separate societies is based on the judgment of the law.

The Failures of Society

Probably the only persons alive today who would not be aware that their social system is insecure would be some as-yet undiscovered tribe in one of the jungle areas of the globe. Surely in our own nation everyone has some sense that the entire fabric of the way we get along with each other is under severe stress. Maybe this is the way it has always been. Yet there is a note of despair evident in the land that may be new. Never before have we been so immediately and intensely aware of what is going on everywhere in our world. Up to this point in history men in despair have been able to fantasize about some new land, some as yet undiscovered paradise, some mythical land of peace and beauty.

We can't do that anymore. We cannot dream of cities of gold or fountains of youth or island kingdoms peopled with noble, gentle savages. We know that there are no gardens of Eden anywhere in our world. We do know that everywhere in our world there is chaos, strife, cruelty. There are no more sanctuaries left. No place to flee from our failure to find out how to live in peace with each other.

We are alone in the universe and we know it.

I am alone in the darkening jungle.

The sense of failure and aloneness might be manageable if we had some hopes for a way out. Right now, after several thousand years of recorded history, we know that every prophet who claimed to have a human way to peace has been a false prophet. Look at the record:

> Science and technology have failed.
> Education has failed.

Democracy, communism, fascism, and monarchy have failed.

Anarchy and nihilism have failed.

Art, music, and literature have failed.

Emotion and reason have failed.

The "common people" have failed.

The intelligentsia have failed.

Affluence and plenty have failed.

Humanism and enlightenment have failed.

Evolution has failed.

Psychoanalysis and psychology and philosophy have failed.

Evil has failed.

Religion has failed.

War has failed.

Love has failed.

Over five thousand years of history — a history of failure to find peace. Name any factor, any ability, any direction, any discipline, any hope. All have been tried. All have failed. Thus it will ever be so long as men live only under the demand of the law to-be-what-they-are-not and not-to-be-what-they-are. So long as the process of measurement and evaluation of self and others set up by that demand remains intact, it simply does not matter what specific activity, emotion, cognition, technique, or program is advanced as the path to peace among men. Be it love or hate, reason or experience, pluralism or segregation, or any other thing, the end result will be the same — prejudice.

In Dostoevsky's *The Brothers Karamazov*, Father Zossima makes a comment which conveys the essence of living only under the law. "Fathers and teachers, I ponder 'What is Hell?' I maintain that it is the suffering of being unable to love."

6

I Search for a Group to Heal My Hurt

My hurt leads me to search for personal identity, for a good opinion of myself, in love and community. It seems right to have a warm and affectionate regard for persons like me.

From the beginning philosophers and kings, carpenters and bureaucrats alike have asked, "How do we create a good community and avoid disorder?" The promise of community has frequently taken this form: "Join with us and submit to our authority and you shall be free, secure, and happy." It is not apparent in this attractive and tempting offer, but if we accept it, we initiate a process that destroys our identity and freedom.

The Search for a Protective Community

Jerry had first come to my office when he was 12 years old. His family was severely shaken by the suicide of the father. The mother thought Jerry needed to work through any possible effects of this event. Jerry was an outstanding 12-year-old, sharp, talented, and likeable. He coped admirably with the tragedy. Following this period Jerry came to "check in" about once a year.

Jerry grew strong and straight. His hair did also. He identified with the youth counter culture, with rock music, freedom of action, caring relationships, anti-war sentiments, and the new politics. He experimented moderately with drugs but avoided "hard" drugs.

I last saw Jerry at the age of 18. He was more disturbed than I had ever seen him. He had been picked up in a western state for hitchhiking. He was eventually freed after two days in jail. However, while in jail, his hair had been cut. He was angry about this, of course, but what really disturbed him was what happened after he got home.

Before his hair had been shorn, Jerry had been quite comfortable and happy in his group. With his long hair, tie-dyed jeans, and boots, he experienced community. He could strike up conversations, share "joints," join in music experiences freely with persons whom he had never seen before. They were like him and he was like them.

Only one thing had changed about him. He now had short hair. When he approached a "long hair" on the street, he met distrust and coldness. People turned away from him. Girls rejected him. He had a hard time trying to buy some marijuana. He went into hiding until his hair grew back. That is when he came to see me again. He did not know what to do. He could understand why the "straights" cut his hair. They were different and he knew he didn't fit there. He could not understand how his own group rejected him. He said, "I found out that the 'long hairs' are just like the 'short hairs.'" He felt betrayed. He felt he could not trust any group or person again. This young man had been able to handle the suicide of his father at age 12. He could not cope with the failure of his group to deliver on the promise of a secure place for him. He said, "All I have now is my guitar. That's all I do — play my guitar."

Jerry's experience is really a common human experience. Like Jerry, I identify a group of people like me, put trust in it, and do not find the promised freedom and security. The group, like me, stands under accusation. It, too, is not what it ought to be, nor can it be what it is. The group, too, must measure and evaluate. It has norms, rules, expectations which I must meet. I do not succeed there either. I am aware of the inadequacies of my attempts to meet the evaluations of the group.

John fretted about his clothing. He did not have the knack of dressing the way a banker should dress. Terry was impotent. He could not accept the norms of the wife-swapping group he and his wife were in. Yet he believed he should be able to join the activities freely. There was something wrong with him that he could not do so. Martha is nervous about how her circle group will react to her carefully prepared Bible study. Shirley planned and labored for two weeks. On Christmas day, with everything else ready, she set the plate of turkey on the table before her husband's family and collapsed. She spent the remainder of the day in bed. The family still teases her about it.

That is the way it works. I look for identity and

strength in a group of people like me. It seems to be a way to meet the demand of the law. But then I am dependent on the norms of the group of people like me to establish the acceptable range of behaviors. When I do not fit within those norms, I am judged.

Living only under the law means that I must seek security through the group. The paradox and futility is that when I try to escape the accusation of the law through being part of a group, I am merely submitting to another form of accusation. I look to a group to give me personal identity. To be in the group I must surrender individuality, the very object of the search.

Law orientation must seek out a protective community of men who reinforce each other through a collective uniformity of behavior. It is a false reasoning. The effect of that false reasoning is described by Sartre in a passage that is worth quoting in full.

> How can one choose to reason falsely? It is because of a longing for impenetrability. The rational man groans as he gropes for the truth; he knows that his reasoning is no more than tentative, that other considerations may supervene to cast doubt on it. He never sees very clearly where he is going; he is 'open'; he may even appear to be hesitant. But there are people who are attracted by the durability of a stone. They wish to be massive and impenetrable; they wish not to change. Where, indeed, would change take them? We have here a basic fear of oneself and of truth. What frightens them is not the content of truth, of which they have no conception, but the form itself of truth, that thing of indefinite approximation. It is as if their own existence were in continual suspension. But they wish to exist all at once and right away. They do not want any acquired opinions; they want them to be innate. Since they are afraid of reasoning, they wish to lead the kind

of life wherein reasoning and research play only a subordinate role, wherein one seeks only what he has already found, wherein one becomes only what one already was. This is nothing but passion. Only a strong emotional bias can give a lightning-like certainty; it alone can hold reasoning in leash; it alone can remain impervious to experience and last for a whole lifetime. . . .

This man fears every kind of solitude, that of the genius as much as that of the murderer; he is the man of the crowd. However small his stature, he takes every precaution to make it smaller, lest he stand out from the herd and find himself face to face with himself.

This is a clear description of what it means to live only under the law. Sartre includes all of the elements — resistance to change, solid social structures, prejudice, and need for absolutism — that we have located in law orientation. But he does not escape the law and its demands. He sets up the way-to-be — the "open" man of reason subscribing to tentativeness and research. When I read this quotation I think, "Yes, I should be reasonable. Yes, I don't want to be the way I am, closed and unreasonable." As soon as Sartre describes the way he feels a man ought to be, "open" and reasonable, that becomes the standard, the yardstick. The process of measurement and evaluation is instantaneously in effect. You or I or anybody else can immediately measure ourselves and others as to how "open" or how reasonable we are being. When I have that assessment fixed, then I can and do engage in self-blame or blaming others. The pain of living only under the law remains.

The Need for Absolutism

Jeanette is a petite housewife of 26. She has two young children. Her husband is a master plumber. Jeanette is pious and faithful. Her congregation and her involvement in it are very important to her. At a Bible study group Jeanette's pastor began to talk about the charismatic movement. He believed in the baptism of the Spirit, prophesying, healing, and speaking in tongues. At one group session he talked about demons and Satan and casting them out of possessed persons. He said that Satan's prayer was "God be damned!"

At home that afternoon Jeanette found this phrase, "God be damned!" running through her mind. She suddenly realized that *she* was saying it. Jeanette was horrified. All of her piety, all of her certainty, all of her sense of belonging to a congregation disappeared.

Jeanette became very nervous, distraught, and frightened. Her life, which had been pleasant and serene, became hell overnight. When Jeanette finally sought help three months later, she was literally ready to commit suicide. Her need for absolute, rigid, firm attitudes, and close identification with her group could not tolerate even the slightest deviation. When she found herself repeating what she had been told was a prayer to Satan, she thought she had become Satan's servant. There was no other possibility. Jeanette cannot conceive of any ambiguity in her life.

John T. is a competent bio-statistician. His wife and children live in constant fear and tension. John also needs absolute, firm, and sure beliefs and attitudes. For him it is simply not possible to tolerate any imprecision. The way it works out in his family life is evident in what happened one night. John had come home feeling expansive and good. A quiet dinner out with his wife and children had been planned for some time. At the table John idly asked his wife if she had paid a particular bill. She had not. Even though it was not overdue, John's response was, "That is absolutely irresponsible!" The evening ended with John taking his family home before they finished their meal. His wife was quietly sobbing. The children were confused and frightened. John rested secure in his conviction that he was right.

These illustrate how the need for absolutism affects daily life. Relationships with other persons are difficult and frequently unrewarding. Self and others are fit into neat little boxes. No ambiguity or blurring of borders between the boxes is allowed. If a thing is so, it is so. Period. That's all there is to it. The difficulty created by application of absolute standards is that neither persons nor human life as such fit neatly into boxes. We keep trying and trying to cram ourselves and people around us into our neat, trim categories. But it does not work.

Every human act is fundamentally ambivalent. The very same act through which I reach out to caress you with tenderness is also potentially an aggressive one. I can reach out to smite you with violence as well. Try to put a man into a box and he will find some way to confound you. Even God who created man would not keep man in a box. He did not compel Adam and Eve to remain in the Garden.

Joan A. is in her middle 30s. Joan has two separate personalities. One is loving, caring, and beautiful. The other is hateful, vicious, and ugly. The hatred is directed against her husband. I advised her to enter a hospital. When I saw Joan and her husband together they refused hospitalization for Joan. The husband insisted that they "were one." If Joan was sick, he was sick. He allowed no separation between his own personality and Joan's. She was he and he was she. That night there was a violent upheaval. Joan went to the hospital. When next I saw them together the husband tried to repeat his performance of totally incorporating Joan into his life, all done in the name of love.

Suddenly Joan leaned forward and in a very calm and reasonable voice said the following. "George, I have kept the vows I made when we married. I have borne your children. I have gone where you have gone on your jobs. I have helped you financially by working. I cook your meals, wash your clothes, and love you whenever you want. Now! You must let me have my own sickness! You cannot take that away from me, too. I will have my own sickness!"

Dostoevsky wrote, "Out of sheer ingratitude, man will play you a dirty trick just to prove that men are still men and not the keys of a piano. . . . And even if you could prove that a man is only a piano key, he would still do something out of sheer perversity — he would create destruction and chaos just to gain his point. . . . And if this could in turn be analyzed and prevented by predicting that it would occur, then man would deliberately go mad to prove his point."

Living only under the law leads to absolutism imposed on life and person. It does not work. People will not fit into boxes.

What the Group Provides

The group of persons like me that I identify with is granted absolute qualities. Its standards, yardsticks, and measuring process is accepted, given an authoritative position in my life, and regarded as a source of certainty. I think that I know who I am because I know about my group, the others like me.

Now, what else does the group give me?

The group I have identified as mine supports and legitimizes the entire absolute, rigid set of rules and measurements that make up my way of life. I am not fully aware of all of the ways in which my group supports my way of life. Many of them are very subtle. I may not be aware that the way I hold my cigarette, light it, flick ashes from it, and grind it out or flip it away is determined by my group. I become aware of it when I suddenly feel out of place in a group where they do the whole thing differently. Then I may become vaguely uncomfortable without being quite sure why. Add up more subtle cues like that and we have a base for the anxiety and inadequacy felt by many persons when they are in a strange or new group. They don't know all the rules for that group. "What will they think of me?"

As pastor I once asked a competent, responsible man to serve as an officer of the congregation. He was about 30, a carpenter and rancher. The parish was located in a university town. A large number of the members were connected with the university or nearby research facilities. The carpenter/rancher refused to take any leadership responsibility. He said, "The congregation is a 'silk stocking' church. I really don't fit in. I can't be an officer." He was willing to work in other ways and did. He could go hunting with me. He was faithful in church attendance and generous in giving money. He could not be an officer in the face of what he felt were the group rules of the educated white-collar professional.

Positively, the group I identify with serves to support what I believe in and what I view as the good way of life as expressed in these statements:

> You can tell if a person is a real Christian or not.
>
> Unity among Christians can come only after complete doctrinal agreement.
>
> As far as the real questions that I wrestle with are concerned, the Church generally provides answers that are helpful.
>
> When I attend worship services I am among friends.
>
> Most of my friends would feel welcome at any service or meeting in my congregation.
>
> A person who does not believe in God should not be permitted to teach in a church-related college.
>
> Church-supported welfare and service agencies do a better job than similar state or private agencies.
>
> Church-supported colleges do a better job than comparable state or private schools in teaching academic subjects like math, history, and biology.
>
> Religious education in schools should be compulsory.

Taken individually, some of these statements are acceptable. Taken together as a whole, and fit into the context of the resistance to change, reliance on rigid rules and structure, and an absolute view of religion and life, they demonstrate the reliance on the group which is characteristic of living only under the law.

In a little mountain town two bar/restaurants are

separated only by a small parking lot. A large group of counter culture advocates took up residence in this old mining town inhabited by one hundred permanent residents and several hundred summer visitors. While there were some troubles, the disparate residents have worked out a way of living together. An integral part of that accommodation is the existence of these two separate but equal establishments. One is for the "straights," the old-timers, the summer visitors from the suburbs of the midwest. The other is for the commune types, the youthful hitchhikers, the anti-war, pro-new-politics groups. Each place serves as a community center for one group.

On a given night you can see a family pull into the parking lot in a Lincoln Continental. The well-dressed suburbanites go into one bar for a meal of steak or shrimp, soft music, cocktails, served by middle-aged waitresses in black uniforms. They get the latest gossip about the activities of the other group and the countermeasures of their own group.

Immediately after them a beat-up VW bus pulls into the lot. It is rusty, smoking, hand-painted with flowers and slogans. Several people dressed in jeans, beads, Indian boots, old overalls, pile out followed by a St. Bernard. They go into the other bar. They have a meal of hamburger, garbanzo beans, organically grown vegetables, and drink pop-wines served by young waitresses with braids, jeans, and no bras. They, too, hear about their group and the other group as well, but over the high decibels of rock music.

Both groups need the focal point of these two establishments for support from other persons, for validation of their distinct ways of life. Without these two temples there would likely be open warfare. Both groups show the basic effect of living only under the law and the resultant need for a collective group that enforces uniformity of behavior and measurement processes.

Comfort Is a Warm Group

Living only under the law puts a person in the impossible bind of needing to-be-what-he-is-not and needing not-to-be-what-he-is. A group offers support in our attempts to defend against that impossible situation. A group, however, is also exploited or used in other ways. There is a need for some kind of good feeling to avoid the pain of the constant accusation. The dimensions of law orientation include an exploitative attitude toward the group. It helps me feel good, even if only momentarily, and gets me some personal advantages.

> One reason for my being a church member is that such membership helps to establish a person in the community.
> The purpose of prayer is to secure a happy and peaceful life.
> We should be concerned with our own private welfare and stop trying to help others by butting into their private lives.
> The more liberally I support my congregation financially, the closer I feel to it and to God.
> If one will only grasp God's grace and trust in his love, all doors will be opened and all obstacles will melt away.
> Knowing Christ as Lord brings complete happiness no matter what.

Individual statements may reflect a desirable attitude. Taken as a whole and in the context of law orientation they illustrate the selfish using of the group for my own purposes, including feeling good, soft, warm, and sentimental.

Doris was one of the original "red-hot mamas." She was 5'4", weighed 321 pounds, and could belt out a torch song in a throaty, husky voice that was a parody of sexuality. She was good at it. She had sung and danced in shady cabarets for several years. When I saw Doris she was looking for a way to get rid of her third husband while trying to keep two lovers happy and ignorant of each other. She also had a variety of vague, non-specific physical problems. Doris had been "confirmed Lutheran" and firmly held to her conviction that she was a highly religious person. She would cry readily while talking of her faith and break into a torch rendition of "Just as I Am" or "In the Garden." While her mascara made sooty tracks down her pudgy cheeks and around her cupid's bow mouth, Doris repeated all of the clichés about faith and trust in God, about the church, and about how nice it felt to pray, sing, and worship.

Doris used everybody and everything for her own purposes. This included the church and her religion. Yet she is a likeable person. She is so unabashed and enthusiastic about it all, there is a certain charm that comes across. It works for Doris, too. She really does feel good for a short time. But, when that passes, her manipulativeness and anger come back to the forefront until the next time she needs to feel good when somebody is frustrating her desires.

Warren is a Ph.D. psychologist. He is heavily involved in human awareness, growth, and development. He has a meditation room in his house with carpeted floors, walls, and ceilings. His publication list is quite lengthy. He has some national recognition. Warren is quite disdainful of his background in a conservative Christian church. He regards himself as liberated from that foolishness. Now he lights incense and candles while meditating in the lotus position. He feels good and claims much refreshment and revitalization from this practice.

At the same time Warren has a reputation as a young psychologist on the way up. He is quite careful to invite into his home and meditation room only those persons who can do him some good in his climb up. He is not averse to affairs but only with women who can advance his career. His behavior toward superiors and peers is impeccable. His teaching, on the other hand, is done largely by teaching assistants. He is short, rude, and impatient with students. "You do not gain advancement by being a good teacher," he says.

Doris and Warren are both exploiters and manipulators. Both live only under the law. Both seek support and comfort for their own personal needs from the group they identify with as theirs. Of the two, Doris is the more likeable, though Warren is by far the more intelligent. Both illustrate the way in which we use the groups we belong to for our own purposes. This is the inevitable result of living only under the law.

The Group Is Fine, But . . .

Living only under the law requires a group for support, for common rules and yardsticks, and offers opportunity for personal payoff. However, a curious element of disregard for all of that is also a part of law orientation. These statements are a part of the dimension of self-oriented utilitarianism as well.

> Sometimes it's all right to get around the law if you don't actually break it.
> In times like these a person ought to enjoy what he can *now* and not wait.
> I accept most easily pressures to close one's eyes to dishonest behavior.

How is it possible for persons living only under the law, showing high need for rigid, absolute, and unchanging social structures, placing great importance on group-supported rules, also to be quite willing to break laws, customs, and morals for the sake of immediate gratification of personal desires?

The examples cited in this and the preceding chapters illustrate the inevitable pain of living only under the law. Pain is the consequence of being caught in the vice of meeting the demand to-be-what-I-am-not and not-to-be-what-I-am. Try as I will, I cannot escape that pain when all I hear is, "It is not enough!" I try the route of external rules and putting authority in groups of people like me. I try to look good by putting down groups that are different from me. I seek the comfort and emotional support of a group while exploiting it for my own desires. None of it works! Life still feels like hell! It still hurts!

If hell is to hurt, I rationalize that heaven must be to feel good, not to hurt. If I am a person living only under the law, happiness and well-being become my goal. For some time now the dominant ideas of man's goals and visions have defined the end state of man as his happiness and well being. Whether it is Freudian psychoanalysis, communist dogma, American pragmatism, or humanism of various stripes, the common theme shared by all is the supreme evaluation placed on "feeling good."

The high value placed on the good feelings of men results in the kind of statement made by Rousseau in *Emile:*

> Such principles of conduct as . . . I must lay down for my guidance in the fulfillment of my destiny in this world. . . . I do not derive from the principles of the higher philosophy, I find them in the depths of my heart, traced by nature in characters which nothing can efface. I need only consult myself with regard to what I wish to do; what I feel to be right is right, what I feel to be wrong is wrong.

"Doing your own thing" is hardly a new philosophical or moral insight. Rather it comes naturally when an individual experiences the failure of the structures, rules, and groups that he has trusted to give him personal identity. All that there is left to do is to try to find happiness and well-being in any way possible. Therefore, "get yours while the getting is good."

If I live only under the law, I try to find support for myself in groups. I look to groups to give me identity and security. I experience the futility of this dependence on groups. It does not work. Life still feels like hell. In frustration and anger I turn to immediate gratification of my desires, hoping that I will feel good. My own feelings become the only guide to my behavior. The result is the curious phenomenon that although I am very rigid and rule-oriented, I break out fairly readily into acts of dishonesty or immorality. This might be called the "Saturday night syndrome." Work hard, keep the rules, stay close to home, but Saturday night is the night to howl.

7

The Harder I Try, the Worse It Feels

Salvation by Works and Pessimism are two more dimensions of law orientation. The meaning of these elements in understanding the pain of living only under the law is not difficult. Nevertheless, the peculiar poignancy of living only under the law is more clear here than in some of the other dimensions and statements of law orientation.

When living only under the law is expressed in religious terms, the fundamental system of measurement and evaluation set up by the law written in men's hearts makes a religion of belief in the saving power of works inevitable. The only God the man living only under law knows is a God who measures. What is measured is the man himself. The self, the being of man, does not really exist for the law-oriented person. The self is lost in between the demand to-be-what-you-are-not and not-to-be-what-you-are. The one thing left to offer to the God who measures is the things that I do, whatever they may be.

Law orientation does this. The statements that reflect the conviction that God measures the works done are the following:

> Sin is whatever people (society) think is wrong behavior.
>
> Being tolerant means that one accepts all religions — including Christianity — as equally important before God.
>
> God is satisfied if a person lives the best life he can.
>
> Salvation depends upon being sincere in whatever you believe.
>
> The main emphasis of the Gospel is on God's rules for right living.
>
> A person at birth is neither good nor bad.
>
> If I say I believe in God and do right, I will get to heaven.
>
> Although there are many religions in the world, most of them lead to the same God.
>
> The Bible teaches that God is like a friendly neighbor living upstairs.
>
> Hard work will always pay off if you have faith in yourself and stick to it.
>
> Hard work keeps people from getting into trouble.
>
> A man should stand on his own two feet and not depend on others for help or favors.
>
> There is nothing which science cannot eventually understand.

A person who tells you *all* of these statements about his beliefs is clearly telling you that his view of religion is basically one of measurement. He has looked at religions, measured them, and he tells you they are all the same. He sees no difference between the religions. They are all the same, not only because they all lead to the same place, but primarily because they all are simply measurement processes. All religions set up the system of telling you "Do this and then you are good; do this and then you are bad."

For the law-oriented person, that is literally true. That is what he experiences. In all of his life, he finds that he is measured and he measures himself. Everything that happens to him, inside and outside, tells him that. He simply has no contrary information.

This is crucial in understanding the pain of living only under the law. There appears to be no way out of it. The person living only under the law is not deliberately or volitionally choosing that way of life. It is the only way there is for him. He is desperately struggling to make sense out of life as he knows it. The way it makes sense is as a lifelong process of measurement.

In religious terms, the law-oriented person correctly observes that all the religions *he knows* are religions of law. As far as he knows, he is right when he says they are all the same. He is right when he says they all lead to the same place. Take a person who belongs to a Christian church. If he indeed believes that "The main emphasis of the gospel is on God's rules for right living," then he knows Christianity, too, only as a religion of law. For him, it is like every other religion in the world. They all tell you what you must do to be good and what you must not do to avoid being bad.

It is not surprising that a person living only under the law believes all religions to be the same, to lead to the same place, and believes that it all depends on what you do or don't do. At the level of the law, that is the way it is. Furthermore, so long as an individual is living only under the law, he is going to see and hear only that which supports him in his present law-oriented beliefs. His perception of sermons, Bible passages, religious conversations, and the like, is limited to perception of the message of the law: "You are not what you ought to be!" Every bit of information that comes to him is shaped and molded into confirmation of what he already knows — only the law.

All of us tend to want to continue to believe what we have accepted as true. When any doubt is cast on our assumptions, we will seek all manner of excuses for clinging to them. The result is that most of our reasoning and dialog is finding arguments for continuing to believe as we already do. Recent research establishes that this process of maintaining our beliefs leads even to actual perceptual distortion. We literally do not see or will distort information that is discrepant with our beliefs. This makes the pain of living only under the law extremely difficult to escape. The trap is strengthened by the human tendency to maintain and defend whatever the present belief system is.

Studies of perception suggest that persons living only under the law literally see and experience their world differently from persons not so stringently controlled by the law. Persons who were rigid, authoritarian, markedly prejudiced, and resistant to change have been shown not to be able to tolerate ambiguity in visual perception.

In one experiment, a picture of a dog was followed by several other pictures which gradually changed to a picture of a cat. The rigid, authoritarian group (law-oriented) saw the transitional picture as a dog much longer than a group not as rigid and authoritarian. The same intolerance of ambiguity was found when, instead of animal pictures, the persons saw a gradually changing series of numbers.

People also differ in the ways in which they maintain their orientation in space. Persons who are relatively passive, low in self-esteem, ready to submit to external authority, lacking in awareness and acceptance of self and others (characteristics of a law orientation) relied much more heavily on external visual surroundings. They distorted their perceptions more seriously than persons able to accept cues from their own bodies (e.g., gravitational cues).

The suggestion that persons living only under the law literally perceive their world in a given fashion is extremely important. For anyone who wishes to understand what it means to live only under the law, this is crucial. It means that in many subtle but crucial daily experiences the person who knows only the law literally sees and feels a different world than a person with some measure of freedom from the demand of the law. All of the ramifications of this are difficult to comprehend. For one thing, it makes it more difficult to ascribe deliberate, volitional malice to some of the less desirable effects of living only under the law (e.g., prejudicial attitudes).

Achievement

Along with the experience that all religions are the same, that is, religions of law, and the perceptual effects, there is a high stress upon achievement when one lives only under the law. Remember these statements that are part of belief in salvation by works:

> Hard work will always pay off if you have faith in yourself and stick to it.
>
> Hard work keeps people from getting into trouble.
>
> A man should stand on his own two feet and not depend on others for help or favors.

This is one of the most common ways people try to find a way out of the bind of the law that you cannot-be-what-you-are and must-be-what-you-cannot-be. If only I achieve, work hard, succeed at something, then I will be a good person.

It does not work.

Joe and Martha had worked hard for over 30 years. Joe taught school while Martha worked as a secretary. They saved their money, bought property, and built apartment houses. Martha quit her job when she was 55 and Joe was 57. They built their dream house by the lake at a cost of $100,000. Now they had it made. They could live happily ever after.

Within six months Martha was sitting across from me, wringing her hands, crying, and describing a deep depression. She was unable to sleep, eat, clean her dream house, or keep the accounts. It turns out Joe has a spastic colon, drinks stomach remedies like soda pop, and can't understand what's wrong with Martha.

James came to therapy because he felt he was constantly failing. Objectively, he had his Ph.D. in physics at age 23. He had played college football, baseball, and basketball well enough to have a pro contract offered him. Three years after his degree he was well on the way to becoming one of the nation's leading physicists.

He saw himself as a phony. The more he received praise and honors, the worse he felt. He said, "I waste so much time. I could be doing so much better. Just today I sat in my office and just stared out of the window and did not get anything done. I'm just a hypocrite."

President Lyndon Johnson reached the pinnacle of human accomplishment. He was the most powerful man in the world. He was wealthy. At the reformed 1972 Democratic convention his picture was not displayed with other presidents. His name was never mentioned. He ended his life sitting by the Pedernales striving to justify his record in his memoirs.

The expectation that hard work and dedication will eventually result in a real experience of accomplishment that will satisfy the demands of the law is sure to fail. Nothing succeeds like success in creating the appetite for more and greater success. The more you succeed and the more you achieve, the greater your need for these experiences.

Each time you lean back, ready to relax and enjoy the good feeling of accomplishment, the voice of law whispers, "It is not enough!" Zing! Off and running again. Each time with a greater fear of failure and a greater probability of failure.

The individual or the society basing life on achievement has the paradoxical but inevitable effect of producing his or its own downfall. The sense of potency is converted into a desperate sense of impotency. The result is alienation from self, society, and others.

Pessimism

The last dimension of a law orientation is pessimism. The man living only under the law makes the following statements:

These days a person must look out for himself since there is no one else to depend on for help.

To get ahead today you sometimes have to be bad as well as good.

You have to be a little bit bad to make money these days.

Old people demand more consideration than they have any right to expect.

There is little chance to get ahead on a job unless a man gets a break.

An experienced person knows that most people can't be trusted to be honest in their personal relationships.

There is little one person can do to make the world a better place in which to live.

The alienation from society, from others, and from self that is the inevitable consequence of living only under the law is crystal clear in these statements.

At first glance it seems inconsistent that many of the same persons who are committed to achievement through hard work will also express this kind of pessimistic alienation. But it happens that way. Human beings are not logically consistent, but psychologically consistent. In this case these two dimensions, both established as part of law orientation by rigorous scientific methods, dramatically present the pain and anguish of living only under the law. The harder I try, the worse it feels.

The increase in violence, crime, and psychopathy in our society has caught the attention of every major social critic for the last two decades. The self-destructive character of any society or any individual life based only on the law is becoming increasingly clear in the actual events occurring around us right now. The aim of the whole of Western society since the advent of the Renaissance has been to build a comfortable life, equal distribution of wealth, peace, stable democracy, and, more recently, happiness through successful adjustment. The very country that has come closest to this aim, ours, shows the most severe signs of stress and psychological pain.

The cause is the law. It is the way in which God deals with the world. It is all that the world by itself knows. There is nothing else. Throughout history men who know only the law have desperately tried to build their lives and their societies under the impossible demand to be-what-they-cannot-be and not-to-be-what-they-are. To date, history records failure. We are in the midst of another failure.

The thesis is that men respond to the demand by attempting to conform, to measure up. This sets up the system and process of measurement described earlier. The actual experience is that we do not measure up. This felt discrepancy produces psychological tension. Frustration is inevitable when the experience is that all efforts prescribed by the law fail. Alienation and violence follow. All that remains is a retreat to anarchy, delinquency, and open mutiny. Humanity becomes irrational, society totalitarian, and man's creativity turns to destruction. The demonic is unveiled.

In such a society the regular rebellion of the young is no longer a creative source of social change and is instead nihilistic, pathological and mutinous. There are three basic modes of violent reaction to the demand of the law. Rebellion calls into question specific values and behaviors prescribed by the law or the society, such as questioning codes of sexual conduct. Revolution tries to replace an institution or structure. Alternate styles of family in a communal setting provide one example. Mutiny simply lusts for sheer destruction without alternatives to replace it. Mutiny is the last resource of the trapped, exhausted human spirit, the cannibalism of a lost lifeboat.

8

The Gospel Heals and Sustains

The demand of the law written in men's hearts lies at the base of the kind of psychological pain of individuals and society described in the preceding chapters. I have tried to explain and clarify how living only under the law inevitably issues in such pain. I have claimed that the violence and terror abroad in society today and throughout history are the consequences of a world under only law. The impossible bind for man and society established by the demand not-to-be-what-you-are and to-be-what-you-cannot-be must result in a sense of impotency and alienation from self and others. In consequence, the impotent man in rage pulls down his house around his ears.

At the level of individual life this is clearly what happened to Eric. He was a weak, passive male. He had two convictions by age 21 for passing crudely forged checks. However, on parole he met and married an attractive woman. They soon had three children. Eric became an apprentice plumber. He worked hard. They bought a small house. He tried desperately to please his wife. She dressed well, if garishly. He had no suit. She went out to movies while he watched the children. He brought her cool drinks while she sunned and he mowed the lawn.

Eric's wife disappeared for three days. When she did return she coolly told him she had been sleeping with a boy friend and intended to do so whenever it pleased her. His job was to support her and the children, to please her, and she would stay with him. Eric did not say much. His wife left with the children to visit her mother for a few hours.

Eric set fire to his house.

He watched it burn. Then he passed a forged check, waited for the police, and quietly went off to prison.

The law renders man impotent. When all attempts to meet the demand have failed, all that is left is the self-destructive rage of impotency. The law cannot help. Only the gospel can heal and sustain

The Promise of the Gospel

What, then, is the gospel? It is the message that Jesus Christ died for our sins and was raised for our justification.

The gospel, like the law, is a word of God. It, like the law, is connected with events. The law is tied to Mount Sinai. The gospel is bound to Mount Calvary. It, like the law, deals with our lives and behavior. The law always accuses. The gospel always forgives. Both law and gospel are promise. The promise of the law is, "Do this and then you will live!" We have seen how that promise can never be fulfilled, for no man can meet the demand. The promise of the gospel is different. It is the promise that it has been done and that justification and forgiveness are freely offered. Christ is the fulfiller of that promise. Nothing the law may say by way of accusation can annul or cancel the promise of grace and acceptance that God declares to us in Christ.

The contrast between law and gospel is clear not only in what Christ says, but also in what he does. The four Gospels record the activities of Jesus. As might be expected under the law Jesus divides people into two classes, sinners and righteous. But then he does not associate with the righteous, those in his day who claimed to live by the law's demands. Nor does he encourage others to follow their example of faithful adherence to the law. Instead he associates with the sinners and scathingly denounces the "righteous." The path of the law and adherence to it leads only to man's definition of rightousness and not to God's. The promise of the gospel is that God's righteousness is *given* to men; it is not *earned*.

Christ does not coddle the sinners, telling them that their evil behavior does not really matter, that it is their parents' fault or the fault of society. He does not blame their evil on the environment. Rather he makes plain the judgment on the sinner, encourages to recoil from sin, and insists on personal responsibility. Still he sits with them, eats with them, talks with them, and announces forgiveness to them. When Christ sits down with the sinners, they see "the Holy One of God." There is no doubt. They know that they themselves

95

are not holy, but rather the opposite. There is no possibility of any play-acting or pretending to righteousness.

Truth is an inter-human relation. Christ comes as an equal to the sinners as he joins them at table. In experiencing that equality the sinner can no longer tame the law or hide from it. You simply can't fake it in the presence of Christ. But he has become the friend of sinners. He is their equal though he is no sinner. By becoming the equal of sinners he has made them in turn his equals. Christ is not only truth in person. He is also grace in person. We receive grace from him.

The law accuses and threatens punishment.

The gospel forgives iniquities and promises grace.

The New Life Under the Gospel

What is the power of the gospel? In this book we have looked at ourselves and others for examples of what it means to live under the law. Now comes the temptation to keep things symmetrical by giving examples of how persons and lives have been changed by the gospel. That could be done. There are many spectacular instances of radical changes worked in the lives of men by the power of the gospel. The disciples, men like St. Augustine, and many today are changed by the gospel.

Those who know and believe the gospel are distinguished from others not in appearance, dress, manner, nor behavior. The difference is that they are "led by the Spirit" (Romans 8:14). Life under the gospel is life in the Spirit. The Spirit teaches how to pray, how to love, how to walk, how to live, how to possess the gifts of God. Life in the Spirit is freedom, as Paul says in 2 Corinthians 3:17.

How does that happen? How does it work?

For one thing, it does not mean that we will be able to avoid all psychological pain. That would make magic of the gospel. Living under the gospel is a process, not an ideal state. The process of being led by the Spirit continues throughout life.

As a tactical step in the process of living in the Spirit, a first step is to search out the ways in which I am still listening to the accusation of the law. What beliefs and attitudes do I retain that show how I try to crawl back under the tent of the law, away from the freedom of the gospel? I need to look for the ways in which I am still telling myself that I must be perfectly obedient, measure up to the expectations of others, and show my need for firm and solid groups to support me. When I find myself fearing failure, when I hear my children telling me, "Well, we can't all be perfect like you," when I feel anger and blame for a stupid bridge partner, then I know that I am listening to the demand of the law and trying to hide from it. I need to turn back to Christ, the friend of sinners, and hear and receive the grace and truth he alone gives. For that to happen I depend on the Word and the sacraments, preaching and teaching, the ministry of the church, the body of Christ.

What Do I Do?

Nothing.

If I try to set up a schedule of what I must do to live under the gospel, I am immediately caught under the measurement process of the law. Suppose I write out a point-by-point statement of what it means to live under the gospel. You respond by saying to yourself, "Yes, that is the way I should be. I must strive to be that way." You are going to find that you don't succeed. That is the door to despair. If you feel that you do succeed, that is the door to pride and works righteousness.

Every pastor has heard the plaintive cry of despair, "I am not a good enough Christian!" He hears it on death beds, in adult classes, in confirmation classes, in hospitals, over the barnyard fence, through screen doors. Even those most able to verbalize a knowledge of God's gift of grace know that their lives, thoughts, and feelings do not fully show the fruits of the Spirit.

An eight-year-old girl had a particularly warm and good experience with her mother, a truly gentle, gracious, and compassionate woman. They walked gently through the dusk, hand in hand, slowly coming home. There was one of those rare moments of good closeness, tender caring and sharing. Intimate laughter tinkled between them, and eyes melted as the mother prepared her daughter for bed and tucked her in. Later that night the mother looked in on her daughter. She found this printed note clutched in her girl's hand: "Dear God, I try so hard to do what you want but it just doesn't seem to work out. I love you! Betty." The sweet, good emotional release of the evening opened up the pain in this eight-year-old's heart. It is the identical pain of many conscientious and devout Christians.

Surely the Spirit grants gifts and fruits of the gospel. They are the desirable qualities like love, joy, peace, patience. But how do they grow and develop in my life? The growth and presence of the gifts of the Spirit are the work of God's Holy Spirit and the Spirit of Christ dwelling in the heart. They are gifts of God. He and he alone nurtures and supports them in me. They are his doing, not mine.

God's work in me is done through his Word and sacraments. They are the means he uses to lead me through my life and the process of struggling with the tension between law and gospel in my life. What the Word and sacraments bring about in my life is God's choice. There simply is no *one* way for all Christians to live out the meaning of the gospel. There are as many ways, stages, twists, turnings, and combinations of spiritual gifts and growth as there are Christians. God does his work on an individual basis. Since every man is unique, determining the form and shape of the Christian life is an individual process. In the words of Luther, "In Christendom it will not do to issue laws so that there is a general rule pertaining to self-control. For people are not alike. One is strong, another is weak by nature, and no one is always as fit in every respect as the other person is. Therefore, everyone should learn to know himself, what he can do and what he can stand."

My Choice

The choices that I have available and can make without confusing law and gospel are choices that exclude. When I am able to understand the effects of living only under the law, I can choose to resist, to exclude those patterns of behavior. The pattern of relying on external authority is one example. When I see how my life reflects reliance on external authority, I can say "No" to that pattern. I can resist pressures to social conformity, group norms and expectations, and need for approval of others. The growth of my ability to place more reliance on internal authority, my own self, depends on God's doing. As Paul says, "Christ lives in me." As the life of Christ grows in me, my self grows. He feeds and nourishes me.

My Internal World

In my inner world there are mountains and plains, deserts and jungles, ruined cities and decayed temples, regions as sterile and barren as the moon, areas lush and verdant with greenery, places of dark and storm, places of light and tranquility. In these regions of my being, all kinds of creatures roam. Many of these creatures seem as if they came with life itself, that I had nothing to do with creating them. They have with me partly a symbiotic and partly an independent relationship. If I feed them, they grow stronger, some strong enough to take over and rule me. If I refuse to feed them, although they may never vanish they begin to wither and droop and the power ebbs out of them.

Some of these creatures are Despair, Anger, Envy, Greed, Love, Lust, Joy, Murder, Pride, Peace. The creatures of my interior world are many and varied. In Christ I can choose *not* to feed some of them. I can choose *not* to feed Anger, for example. It may never go away, but it will not grow either. Then when God feeds and nourishes Love with the gift of his love, he will not be competing with a large and powerful creature called Anger. "One can weaken and mortify the body with fasting and works, but one does not expel evil lust in this way. Faith, however, can subdue and restrain it, so that it gives room to the Spirit," Luther said.

A Model for Knowing Myself and Choosing Against Sin

A model of a molecule looks like a jumble of balls joined together by sticks. I can look at and study it and come to understand the molecule. When I understand it, I can change it around, combine it with other molecules, add and subtract from it, and alter it. All the time I am thinking of molecules in terms of the model of balls stuck on sticks. The fact is that the model is not the molecule. There is nothing about the real molecule that corresponds to the balls and sticks of the model. What the model does for me is to allow for a grasp of relationship accurate enough for tinkering with the real molecule.

I suggest that the same function of model — clarifying the relationships — for the process of knowing myself in Christ and growing in the gifts of the spirit can be served by confession and absolution. The elements of confession are: (1) In relationship to another person (God or man), (2) I accept personal responsibility for (3) who I am and what I am doing. The elements of absolution are: (1) In relationship to another person (God and man), (2) I am forgiven and (3) who I am is accepted. What I am doing may then change.

In our lives we encounter all kinds of situations, events, persons, and relationships. In all of them, if I follow the model of confession and absolution, I recognize the relationship quality, accept responsibility, and declare my involvement in it to be faulty. With other men the extent to which I am able to stand in confession before them determines the extent to which I can experience acceptance by them. With God, it is different. God never withdraws his love and acceptance from me even if my acts of confession are faulty.

In relationship to other people this means that I will be willing to speak openly of my responsibility, my errors, my perceptions. I will be confessing in every relationship. Nourished by the absolution given by God, I am ready to receive gifts of love and forgiveness from others.

In this way the pain of experiencing the demands of the law is lessened. When I hurt inside, the gospel heals and sustains me.